OOL CARS

ASTON MARTIN

V12 VANTAGE

BY KAITLYN DULING

EPIC

BELLWETHER MEDIA ››› MINNEAPOLIS, MN

EPIC BOOKS are no ordinary books. They burst with intense action, high-speed heroics, and shadows of the unknown. Are you ready for an Epic adventure?

This edition first published in 2025 by Bellwether Media, Inc.

No part of this publication may be reproduced in whole or in part without written permission of the publisher. For information regarding permission, write to Bellwether Media, Inc., Attention: Permissions Department, 6012 Blue Circle Drive, Minnetonka, MN 55343.

Library of Congress Cataloging-in-Publication Data

LC record for Aston Martin V12 Vantage available at: https://lccn.loc.gov/2024002288

Text copyright © 2025 by Bellwether Media, Inc. EPIC and associated logos are trademarks and/or registered trademarks of Bellwether Media, Inc. Bellwether Media is a division of Chrysalis Education Group.

Editor: Rachael Barnes   Designer: Jeffrey Kollock

Printed in the United States of America, North Mankato, MN.

TABLE OF CONTENTS

A SPEEDY EXIT	4
ALL ABOUT THE V12 VANTAGE	6
PARTS OF THE V12 VANTAGE	10
THE V12 VANTAGE'S FUTURE	20
GLOSSARY	22
TO LEARN MORE	23
INDEX	24

A SPEEDY EXIT

The driver slams down the gas pedal on their Aston Martin V12 Vantage. The **V12 engine** growls. The car picks up speed.

4

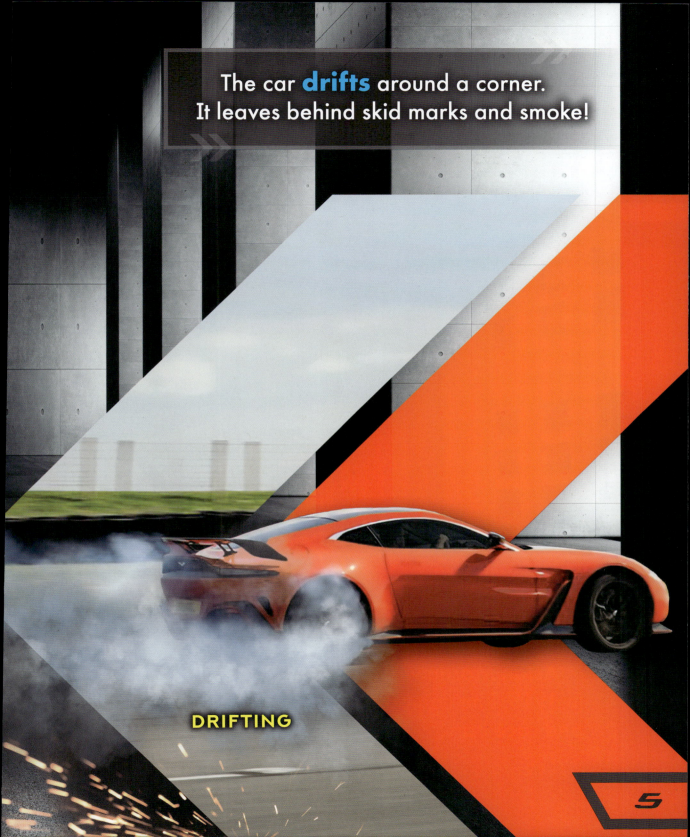

The car **drifts** around a corner. It leaves behind skid marks and smoke!

DRIFTING

ALL ABOUT THE V12 VANTAGE

ASTON MARTIN OFFICES

Aston Martin was founded in England in 1913. The company builds sports cars and race cars.

Many Aston Martin car names start with the letter V. The Vanquish and the Valkyrie are famous **models**.

CRAFTING A CAR
All Aston Martin cars are made by hand!

VALKYRIE

WHERE IS IT MADE?

GAYDON, ENGLAND

EUROPE

The first V12 Vantage was introduced in 2007. It was a **concept car**. The car hit the road as a 2009 model.

There are many **generations** of the car. The 2023 V12 Vantage is the latest.

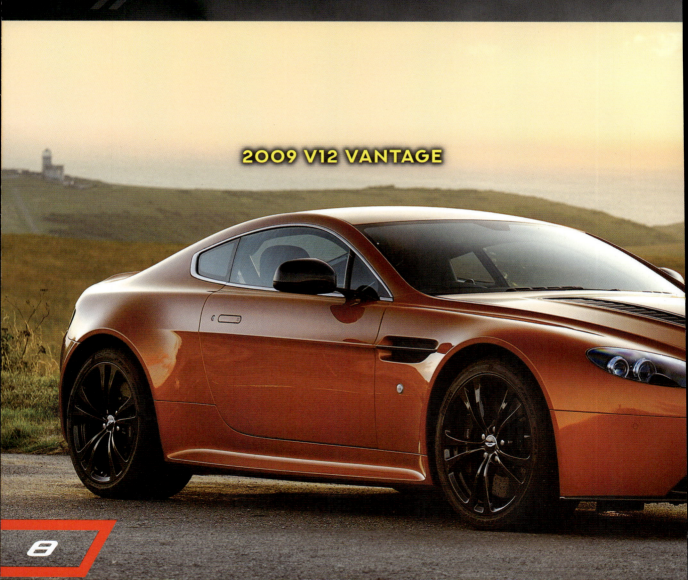

2009 V12 VANTAGE

V12 VANTAGE BASICS

YEAR FIRST MADE — 2009

COST — starts around $300,000

HOW MANY MADE — 333 made in 2022

FEATURES

V12 engine

horseshoe vent

huge grille

PARTS OF THE V12 VANTAGE

The V12 Vantage has Aston Martin's most powerful engine yet. The engine helps the car reach up to 200 miles (322 kilometers) per hour.

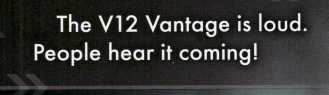

The V12 Vantage is loud. People hear it coming!

The large V12 engine can get very hot. A **horseshoe vent** removes hot air from around the engine.

A huge **grille** lets air move through the car. This cools the engine.

ENGINE SPECS

V12 ENGINE

TOP SPEED — 200 miles (322 kilometers) per hour

0–60 TIME — 3.4 seconds

HORSEPOWER — 690 hp

The V12 Vantage is built to grip the road at high speeds. Its lightweight body is wide and low.

SIZE CHART

WIDTH 85.9 inches (218.2 centimeters)

The **wing** helps move air over the car.

WING

HEIGHT 50.2 inches (127.4 centimeters)

LENGTH 177.7 inches (451.4 centimeters)

15

The V12 Vantage is a two-door **coupe**. Its two seats are low to the ground.

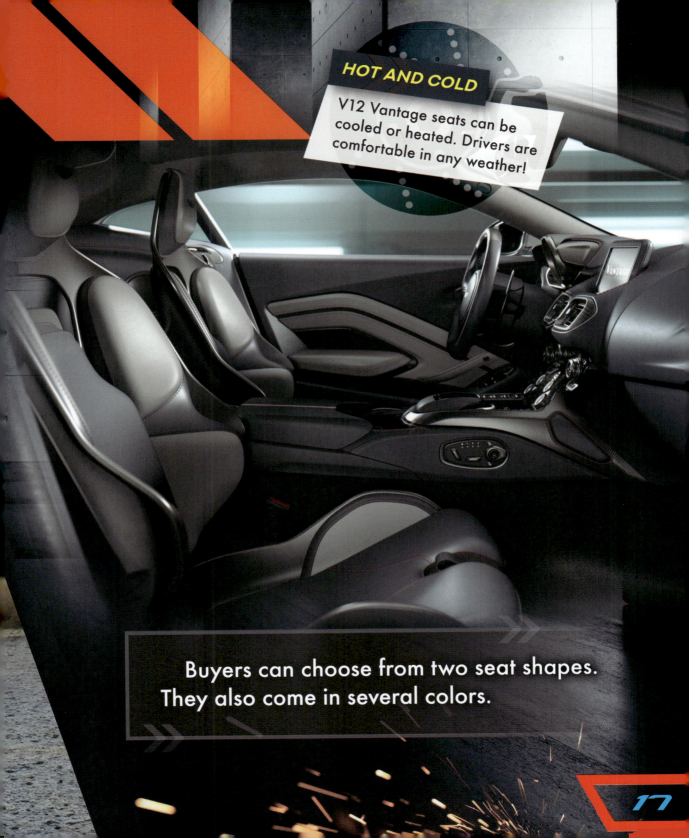

HOT AND COLD

V12 Vantage seats can be cooled or heated. Drivers are comfortable in any weather!

Buyers can choose from two seat shapes. They also come in several colors.

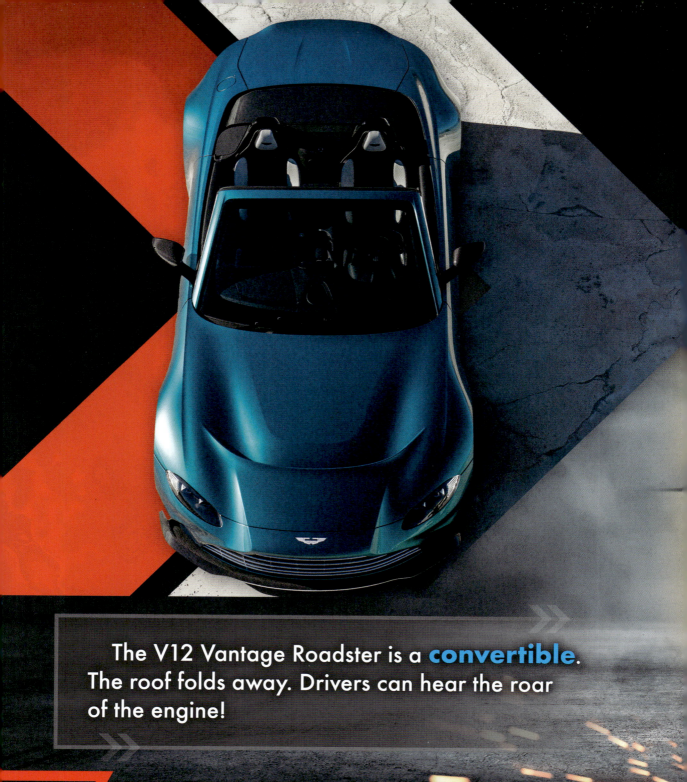

The V12 Vantage Roadster is a **convertible**. The roof folds away. Drivers can hear the roar of the engine!

> The Roadster costs more. Only 249 were made.

ROADSTER

THE V12 VANTAGE'S FUTURE »

The 2023 V12 Vantage was the car's final generation. Aston Martin may build Vantages with other engines.

The company plans to build **electric** cars. They will be fast and better for the planet!

GLOSSARY

concept car—a car built to show a new design

convertible—a car with a folding or soft roof

coupe—a small car with a hard roof that often has two doors

drifts—makes a controlled skid sideways; drifting can leave black tire marks on the road.

electric—able to run without gasoline

generations—specific designs of car models; a generation may last one year or several.

grille—a set of bars that cover an opening on the front of a car; the grille allows air to enter and exit the engine.

horseshoe vent—a U-shaped opening in a car's hood that helps cool the air around the engine

models—specific kinds of cars

V12 engine—an engine with 12 cylinders arranged in the shape of a "V"

wing—a part on a car's body that helps it smoothly travel through the air

TO LEARN MORE

AT THE LIBRARY

Abdo, Kenny. *James Bond's Aston Martin*. Edina, Minn.: ABDO, 2024.

Duling, Kaitlyn. *Aston Martin Valkyrie*. Minneapolis, Minn.: Bellwether Media, 2024.

Sommer, Nathan. *Aston Martin Valhalla*. Minneapolis, Minn.: Bellwether Media, 2023.

ON THE WEB

FACTSURFER

Factsurfer.com gives you a safe, fun way to find more information.

1. Go to www.factsurfer.com.

2. Enter "Aston Martin V12 Vantage" into the search box and click 🔍.

3. Select your book cover to see a list of related content.

INDEX

basics, 9
body, 14
company, 6, 7, 10, 20
concept car, 8
convertible, 18
coupe, 16
drifts, 5
electric cars, 20
engine, 4, 10, 12, 18, 20
engine specs, 12
England, 6, 7
future, 20
generations, 8, 20
grille, 12, 13
history, 6, 7, 8, 20
horseshoe vent, 12, 13
models, 7, 8
names, 7
race cars, 6

Roadster, 18, 19
roof, 18
seats, 16, 17
size, 14–15
speed, 4, 10, 14, 20
sports cars, 6
wing, 15

The images in this book are reproduced through the courtesy of: Damian B Oh/ Wikipedia, front cover; Malcolm Haines/ Alamy, p. 3; Aston Martin/ Car and Driver, pp. 4, 5, 10, 16; Aston Martin/ Aston Martin Media Center, pp. 6, 7, 8-9, 9 (engine and hood), 12, 13, 15 (main and length), 17, 18, 19, 20, 21; Alexandre Prevot/ Wikipedia, p. 9 (isolated); Calreyn88, p. 9 (grille); UK Sports Pics Ltd/ Alamy, p. 11; CJM Photography/ Alamy, p. 14; Mareks Perkons, p. 14 (width).